My Name Is Masak

My Name Is Masak

Alice French

Peguis Publishers
Winnipeg • Canada

Published in hardcover and paperback in 1977
Translated into French and published by Le Cercle du Livre de France Ltée, Ottawa, in 1979
Second reprint, 2002

Printed and bound in Canada

Canadian Cataloguing in Publication Data

French, Alice, 1930–
    My name is Masak

    Autobiographical.
    ISBN 0-919566-55-3 bd.
    ISBN 0-919566-56-1 pa.
    1. French, Alice, 1930–   2. Eskimos–
Northwest Territories.   I. Title
E99.E7F75   971.9′2′030924   C77-002006-2

Cover photo: The author gathers berries on the coast of Hudson Bay near Churchill, Manitoba

Portage & Main Press Ltd.
Formerly Peguis Publishers Ltd.
318 McDermot Avenue
Winnipeg, Manitoba
Canada R3A 0A2

To my children

Listen, listen my children.
And I'll tell you a story of where I was born and
where I grew up.
About your ancestors and the land we lived on.
About the animals and the birds.
So you can see.

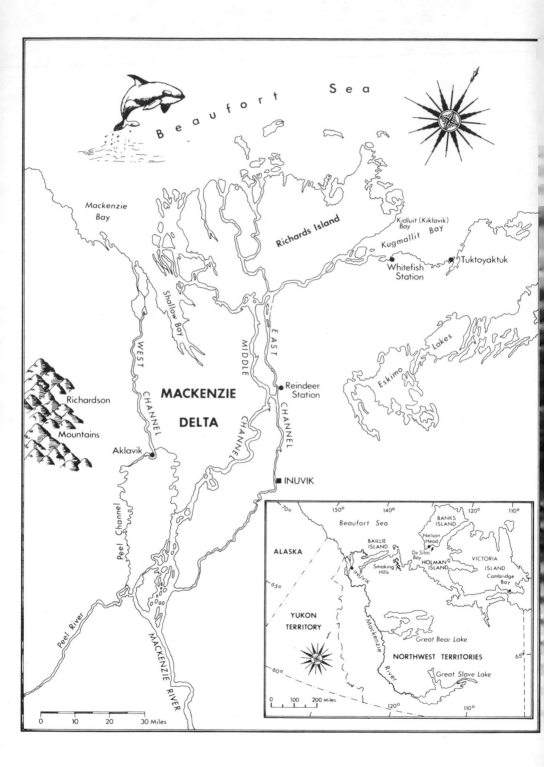

Beaufort Sea

Mackenzie
Bay

Richards Island

Kidluit (Kiklavik)
Bay
Kugmallit Bay

Whitefish
Station

Tuktoyaktuk

Shallow Bay

WEST CHANNEL

MIDDLE CHANNEL

EAST CHANNEL

MACKENZIE

DELTA

Reindeer
Station

Eskimo Lakes

Richardson
Mountains

Aklavik

■ INUVIK

Peel Channel

Peel River

MACKENZIE RIVER

0   10   20   30 Miles

70°   150°   140°   120°   110°

Beaufort Sea

BANKS
ISLAND

Nelson
Head

ALASKA

BAILLIE
ISLAND

De Silas
Bay

HOLMAN
ISLAND

VICTORIA
ISLAND

INUVIK

Smoking
Hills

Cambridge
Bay

65°

YUKON
TERRITORY

Mackenzie River

Great Bear Lake

NORTHWEST TERRITORIES

60°

Great Slave Lake

65°

0   100   200 Miles

120°

110°

Foreword

Alice French's beautiful little book tells the story of her childhood in the Northwest Territories, in the years prior to the Second World War.

People who grew up in the North during this time lived through many changes. I myself started life as a trapper and hunter and went on in turn to become a fur trader, broadcaster, pilot and Member of Parliament. Some people would call this progress. We in the North are not so sure.

Education and communication are fashionable ideas in northern society today. Unfortunately, until recently, education and communication have been one-way streets.

For all his goodwill, the conventional southerner has usually not stopped to listen and learn much about the original people of the Arctic before he began to teach us the ways of his world. Native northerners are now beginning to talk back. They are finally telling other Canadians the way it is and the way it was. Alice French's book is a great contribution to this process.

Our history has been largely written by outsiders and these stories do not often mention people like Alice's family. However, one can never understand the North without getting to know its people. *MY NAME IS MASAK* is one northerner's story in her own words. The North will never be the same again, but Alice's memories will help to keep the recent past alive.

I knew Alice's father, Charlie Smith. I am sure he would be very proud of her and her work, as we all are.

WALLY FIRTH, M.P.,
Northwest Territories

Contents

CHAPTER ONE

Baillie Island

M Y NAME is Masak. I was born in June 1930, on Baillie Island in the Northwest Territories. Baillie Island was quite a big settlement at one time, but now it has washed away into the Beaufort Sea. Not the whole island is gone — just the buildings that once stood on the sandy point: the trading post, the Roman Catholic and Anglican missions, the shack where the Royal Canadian Mounted Police were, and the Eskimos' houses.

My father, Anisalouk, was born and raised in Unalakeet, Alaska. His father was a Laplander; he spoke both English and Eskimo to his family at home, so by the time my father was old enough for school he knew quite a bit of English. School was compulsory in Unalakeet when he was growing up. He went as far as Grade 10.

In 1923 my father came to Herschel Island on the *Nigalik,* the Canalaskan Trading Company ship. From Herschel he went to Baillie Island to work as an interpreter for the police. He added to his wages by doing a bit of trapping.

My mother, Sanggiak, was also an Alaskan Eskimo. She was from the Anaktuvik Pass area. After their marriage my parents settled on Baillie Island. They were known to the white people as Charles and Lily Smith.

At the time I was born, there were many taboos for pregnant women. My mother would be careful how she dressed during this time. If she put something on backwards she might have a backward child. If she put something on inside out, the baby would be born with a skin problem. She did not play string games or make cat's cradles; this would cause her baby to have a cord wrapped around its neck which might strangle it at birth. When she went to bed she always pointed her feet towards the doorway so the baby would know its correct way into the world and not come feet first.

There was no hospital on Baillie Island, so my mother had me at home with an Eskimo midwife to help her. As her time approached she got things ready. She had a fresh caribou skin to kneel on, and scissors and thread for cutting and tying the cord. She did not make clothing and diapers until her baby was born. This would have made her

Baillie Island as it was in the summer of 1929,   H B C
the year before Alice was born.

seem too sure of having a live birth. It would
have been tempting fate to decree otherwise.

After I was born my mother was careful not
to look into a mirror while she was holding me.
She believed, like the other women in the village,
that a baby had special sight and that it might
see things that a grown-up could not see. If I
had seen my reflection in the mirror as a baby
I might have had a distorted view of myself, or
of my mother who held me.

On the day that my mother's labour pains started, she gathered together the things that she would need and placed them under the bed. Then she sent my father out for the midwife. If there were other men or children in the house, she sent them away to visit. Only the women stayed with her. She went about doing her housework as usual, preparing food for the visitors who would be coming to congratulate her and my father afterwards. While my mother and the women waited they drank tea and talked about everything going on in the village. They said nothing about the coming child. It was taboo to speak about the arrival of the baby.

When it was time for the baby to be born, my mother placed the skin on the floor and knelt on it. The midwife knelt behind her and held her around the middle to support her while she pushed the baby into the world. When I was born, the midwife caught me and told my mother that I was a girl. I am sure she hoped I would be a boy. Boys were much preferred over girls. Boys became hunters and provided food for the family. They were also trappers. There was not much a girl could do. She was of little value until she married and brought home a hunter and trapper. And while she was growing up, she had to be

Alice as a child plays near schooners unloading at Baillie Island.

Collection: Alice French

fed and taught how to sew and cook so that she would bring a good man into the family.

In my great-grandmother's time, girls were sometimes left behind to die when they were born. This happened to my great-grandmother. Times were bad and her parents were travelling. They decided that they could not keep her so they put her down on the ground. As they turned to leave, she cried out "Mama," so they picked her up and kept her.

After I was born one of the women went out to tell my father that he had a baby girl. Then he and the other men came in to eat. My mother was already up and working. The other women helped her to spread an oilcloth on the floor and set it with plates and knives and food. Then they all sat on the floor and helped themselves to food and talked about naming me.

At last my parents decided to call me Masak after my father's mother. My Christian name was to be Alice after my mother's mother. During the meal the virtues of both my namesakes were discussed. If I lived up to my namesakes I would make up for being a girl. One of the women took my hands and rubbed them to make sure that I would be a good seamstress. Another went over my eyes so that I would be observant. Still another chewed some food and put it into my mouth so that I would live a long life. The ritual was performed for all children.

For the boy babies there was a different ritual that the men performed. It was much more elaborate. The day after a boy baby was born there was a feast to celebrate his birth. If the father was a good hunter and his position in the social

life of the camps was good, the feast would bring
in visitors from all over the land. The menu for
the feast would include caribou tongue, geese and
ducks, and Eskimo ice cream — a delicacy made
from bone marrow. These things would be eaten
besides the regular fare — rabbits, ptarmigan,
caribou and whale. For the birth of a girl a meal
was enough.

CHAPTER TWO

Family Life at Cambridge Bay

WHEN I was about four, my mother and father took me and my young brother to Cambridge Bay on Victoria Island. My father had accepted a job with the Canalaskan Trading Company, and we travelled to our new home in the Company's ship *Nigalik*. The manager at Cambridge Bay was Captain E. Pasley and my father was to be the interpreter and clerk.

Our house was on Jack's Point, on a high bank surrounded on three sides by water. To the west of us beyond a small river that flowed into the bay, were the RCMP buildings and across the bay to the east was the Hudson's Bay Company post. Cambridge Bay was above the tree line; the building material for our house had been brought in by boat during the summer, along with the food supply. It was a one-room building and when you came into it, you saw the beds ranged along the back wall. The kitchen stove and cupboards were against the front wall, and not quite in the middle of the floor was a coal-burning

The ship 'Nigalik.' It changed hands in 1936 when the Hudson's Bay Company bought the Canalaskan Trading Company.   H B C

heater that warmed the whole house. There were no pictures on the walls; only my father's guns hung on them. One gun was kept near the door always ready for use, for even in the settlement we never knew when a caribou might go by.

I remember one day in the winter, I was looking out of our window when I saw a caribou, its head held up high, running on the sea-ice past our house. It was one of those little white caribou that we see only on the arctic islands. I ran to the store and my mother came right behind me carrying my father's gun.

"There's a caribou down there on the ice," she told him.

He ran to the edge of the little hill that sloped down to the lake and fired a shot. The caribou dropped. My mother and I yelled, "You got him! You got him!" We all ran down the hill towards the animal. Mother and Dad started to skin it. It was a buck in good condition with lots of fat on it. After it was cleaned and quartered, my dad gave some of the meat to the neighbours who by this time had come down to help. When the rest of the meat was carried up to the house, my mom got busy cooking. That night we had boiled tongue, heart, and roasted ribs for supper.

My mother used to go jigging for tomcod in the bay just below our house. Sometimes she walked up to the mouth of the river and tried jigging for char. I went with her on those walks, dressed in my winter clothing. I wore two caribou-skin parkas made from summer skins that had lost their long winter hair. The inside parka was worn with the hair side turned in and the other had the hair side turned out. The hood and cuffs were trimmed with wolverine and my mukluks were made from caribou leggings.

This skin from the legs of the caribou was particularly strong.

Sometimes we would drop in at a friend's snow-house to warm up and have some tea on the way back. I liked to do this. I would play with the other children while the women gossiped. The snow-house would be nice and warm with heat from the soapstone lamp that burned in one corner. We would sit and play on the snow platforms which were covered with furs and used at night for beds.

In the 1930s most of our people were still nomads. They came into the settlement by dog-team at Christmas and Easter to do their trading. When they came at Christmas the ice on the bay in front of our house would become a small village. The men would scramble around, poking at the snow with their snow-knives, looking for just the right type to build their snow-houses. It had to be firm and well packed by the wind so that the blocks of snow could be easily cut. I loved to watch them build their houses. Once the men started to build, it did not take long to complete them. The dogs were tethered around the snow-houses and the sleds were put up against the walls. There was always one big snow-house built for community dances and

A winter camp in the Western Arctic

William Gibson

Eskimo games. The men would make three houses adjoining each other and when they were finished the walls between them would be cut away to make one large room.

The games were arm wrestling, finger pulling,

weight lifting, jumping to see who could go the highest and touch a bone on a string as it was raised higher and higher. There was one game where a straw broom was used. The whisk end of the broom was held against the face with the handle up in the air. Then bending backwards the contestant would touch the floor with the pole end. The pole end would be made shorter and shorter until just a few inches of it showed above the head. The winner was the one who could bend back and touch the floor with the shortest end of the stick without falling.

Outside the big snow-house there were dog-team races, and long-distance running and jumping. There were no prizes for the races and games, but the champions would be known and were challenged the next year.

The games and feasting, visiting back and forth, and playing with lots of children would last about a week. Then one morning I would hear a lot of noise. I would look out the window and see the people loading their sleds and straightening out the harnesses. They were preparing to go back to their camps to live and trap. The dogs would lunge on their chains and bark wildly; they knew that it was time to be on the trail again. As the dogs were being harnessed a few dogfights would break out and the men, using their whips, would untangle dogs and traces. When everything was packed up and the teams ready, the smaller children would be put into their sleeping bags with only their heads showing. The women would climb aboard their sleds and the teams would tear off, happy to be on their way.

It was quiet down on the bay after they left. All we would see were white mounds of silent snow-houses with no one playing outside of them. My mother would tell me not to feel too bad. Easter would be here before we knew it, and all my little friends would be back again.

CHAPTER THREE

Epidemic

ONE WINTER I remember we had a ship staying at the settlement all winter, frozen into the ice in Cambridge Bay. She was called the *St. Roch.* Sometimes we were invited out to the ship for supper, and after supper we would go for a tour around the inside of the ship. The first time I ever saw lantern slides was on the *St. Roch.* They also had something called a view-master. One picture really stuck in my mind — why I don't know. It was of Niagara Falls. I thought that ship must be the biggest one in the world.

When I was five years old we had a bad flu epidemic. To understand how disastrous this or any disease was for us, you have to live among my people. There were no doctors or nurses to help us. The store manager, Mr. Pasley, did as much as he could. He gave us medicine and told us to stay in bed. Some of the people would go outside to try to cool off their fever, but this

15

would only make them sicker than ever. My mother was very ill at this time. She never seemed really well ever again.

After the flu epidemic there were many new graves behind the settlement. It was hard to dig graves, for the permafrost was in the ground all year around. This was the reason the people buried their loved ones on the hill crests, with stones heaped around and on top to keep the animals from disturbing them. Personal belongings were always buried with them so they would have what they needed in the life beyond. The men were laid to rest with their hunting equipment and eating utensils. The women had their cooking pots and lamps and bone needles, and the children had candy and toys.

One day in the spring I and two friends, Mable and June, walked to the grave of a child and took some candy and gum from it. I knew we had done wrong because I could feel the hair rising on the back of my neck. We started to walk very quickly towards our homes, and then we started running as fast as our legs would go. When I got home my mother asked what was chasing me that made me go so fast. I told her about the candy, and she said that we had done a bad thing. She said the graves were sacred, and that

the spirit was still there waiting to be reborn.
That was the first and last time that I ever took
anything from a grave. Most of us believed in
reincarnation; the food and personal belongings
were taken to the graves for the spirit to use while
it awaited the time of rebirth. When a child was
born and given the name of an ancestor, that
spirit was released to live on through his or her
namesake. I was named for both of my parent's
mothers. I was *aga*, their mothers, and I was re-
spected and loved.

In the spring of 1937 when I was seven years
old my father told my brother and me that our
mother had tuberculosis. We would have to go
from Cambridge Bay to the hospital in Aklavik.
So when the Hudson's Bay Company ship came
in with supplies, my father and mother and my
brother, Aynounik, and I, sailed back on it. We
got measles on board and that made my mother
even sicker. I don't know how long it took us
to make that trip but it seemed to last forever.

When we landed at Aklavik my mother went
to the hospital and my brother and I were told
we would be going to a boarding school, whatever
that was. My father tried to explain that a boarding school was where children lived and went
to school. He would not be able to take care of

*Charles Smith with his children Alice (Masak) and Danny (Aynounik)
and a priest from Bathurst Inlet (right).*

Collection: Alice French

us while mother was in the hospital and we would
have to stay there. I did not like the idea. My
brother was only three years old and too young
to understand.

CHAPTER FOUR

Alone

HOW COULD THERE be so many people living in one building? I was so scared that I hung onto my father's hand. I did not like it there and I did not want my father to leave us. There were too many people. My brother was taken away by one of the supervisors. I tried not to cry in front of my father — he felt bad enough as it was.

An Eskimo girl, whose dialect I did not understand, took me to the playroom. She was talking to me in Eskimo, but it did not make sense. Thank goodness she spoke English too. She told me that we were having supper soon. I asked her if I would see my brother. She said yes, at supper time. Then she introduced me to the other girls by my Christian name — Alice. My Eskimo name was not mentioned and I did not hear my name Masak again until I went home.

Then I became aware of different languages. I asked my new friend what dialect the girls were

19

speaking. I was told that it was the language of the Mackenzie Delta and that most of the Eskimo children were from there, except for a few from Coppermine and Cambridge Bay. There were a lot of Indian children from the upper Mackenzie. They were mostly Loucheux with some Dogribs and Slaveys.

Then a white lady came in to tell us it was supper time. Everyone got into line except me. She took my hand and told me her name was Miss Neville. I was taken to one of the lines and told that this would be my place from now on. We marched in single file to the dining-room. Suddenly I saw my little brother. I started towards him, but I was told to stay in line. How little he looked, lost and lonesome. I felt like going over to tell him that everything was going to be all right, only I was not too sure of that myself.

After supper we went back to our side of the school. I did not even get to talk to my brother. We saw each other only at mealtimes. Sometimes we had the chance to shout at each other while playing outside but even outside the boys and girls were not allowed to mix.

Sometime later that fall Reverend H.S. Shepherd, our minister, came to the school to tell me that my mother had died. I did not believe him

All Saints' Anglican Hospital at Aklavik. Alice's mother died in the right wing, ground floor. Her room is marked with an X.

because I had visited her that morning. I went back to the hospital to find her but the bed she had been in was empty. How could she be there one day and not the next? I felt terribly alone. She was the only link I had with home and the life I had been used to. My father had gone back to his trap-line and we would not hear from him for a long time. It was not out of cruelty but out of necessity that he left us.

CHAPTER FIVE

Boarding School

INSIDE THE SCHOOL we had four dormitories on the girls' side. I was in the youngest girls' dormitory for ages six to eight. The dormitories were joined by a big common washroom. There were towel hooks along both walls, wash basins, and jugs of water on a long table. Little brushes and tins of powder were on a shelf built into the middle of the table. I had to wait to see what the other girls would use the little brushes for, so I watched what they did with them as we got ready for bed.

So that was what it was — to brush your teeth with. I wondered what that was supposed to do for you. Somebody told me that it was to keep you from having holes in your teeth. They certainly did have a lot of strange ideas. Another idea was combing your hair with coal oil when you first came to the school. That was to kill the head lice. I didn't have any but we all had to suffer through the coal-oil treatment whether we had lice or not.

Our house mother's name was Annie and she had a room just off the washroom. She told me that my mother was her cousin. That did not mean that I would be favoured above the other girls, but it felt good to know that I had a relative close at hand. She got us off to bed at night and woke us up in the morning.

The staff in our school slept in rooms off the hallway. Downstairs were two big classrooms,

All Saints' Anglican Residential School from the boys' side. The hospital, cathedral and missionary's residence extend along the road to the left.

Anglican Church of Canada Archives

kitchen, staff dining-room, children's dining-room, principal's office, laundry room, a furnace room and two playrooms. The lavatory used to be outside until they had one built into the side of our playroom. The whole of the basement was a storeroom for school supplies and food was kept there, like in a root cellar.

Our days started at seven in the morning. We dressed, washed, and brushed our teeth, made our beds and tidied our dorms. Then we went down to breakfast at eight o'clock.

Breakfast usually was porridge, sweetened with molasses, bread and jam, and tea to drink with sugar and milk. It never varied except on holidays. At nine we went to the classrooms. Then a break for lunch — soup, bread and powdered milk — and back to school again. Supper was the big meal of the day with fish, meat, potatoes, dessert, bread and tea. We had this at five-thirty, usually after a walk around town, or out into the country with our teacher. Bedtime was seven o'clock for the little ones; eight o'clock for the next lot and so on, until the oldest were in bed at ten and the lights were out. I expect it was the same for the boys.

While we were getting ready for bed we talked about the scary stories we would tell after the lights were out. I shivered thinking about them while I brushed my teeth. Betty, standing next to me at the sink, jabbed me in the ribs and scared me half to death.

"Hey Alice," she said. "Did you know that we have a ghost in our dorm? She always sits in the corner combing her hair and you can see the blue sparks flying in every direction." I started to shake because my bed was in one of the far corners of the room.

"Which corner?" I asked in a quavery voice.

"Your corner," she said, and went off to bed.

Then Miss Neville came in and I pleaded with her to tell us a story. As long as she was telling a story the lights would stay on and maybe the girls would go to sleep or be too tired to tell ghost stories.

"Not tonight, Alice," said Miss Neville. "All right, girls, time for bed. No talking after lights out, please."

She looked around to make sure that we were all under our covers and then she turned out the light and closed the door. It sure was dark in there then. I made certain that my bedding was loose so that I could jump out of bed fast if I had to.

Then they began to tell stories. Why did they

always have to be scary ones — reindeer herders taking a coffin creaking through the woods on a sleigh, men reincarnated in dogs, rattling doors and the Devil's cloven hoof-prints on the snow?

Connie, whose bed was closest to the door, was posted as lookout. Her job was to tell us if someone was coming, but she was a most unlikely choice for the job. She talked more than any of us, and often she would forget that she was supposed to be listening for the supervisor's footsteps. As a result we were caught talking and were punished. We had to stand in the corner of the room for half an hour. This got to be very cold, for all we had on was our nightdresses.

One night I was punished in another way for using my bed as a trampoline. I was showing the girls how to go into a standing position from a belly flop. As I came down the bed collapsed to the floor with a crash. Just as I disappeared from view into the bedding, the door opened and there stood Miss Neville.

"What is going on here?" she asked sternly.

There was a silence while I climbed from the ruins of my bed. She came over and grabbed my shoulder and gave me a good shaking.

"Alice, how many times have I told you not to jump on your bed?"

"Many times, Miss Neville," I answered with my teeth rattling in my head.

"That is correct," she said. "For being a naughty and disobedient child you shall sleep in your bed just as it is for a week. Now all of you settle down and no more nonsense."

I climbed into bed and found that it was quite comfortable. In the morning I woke up and realized that I had slept through the night without once waking up because of the cold. By the end of the week I had grown quite attached to my bed on the floor and hated to give it up for another.

Friday night was bath night. All one hundred and twenty-five of us were issued clean bedding and clothing. This consisted of one pair of long underwear, one pair of fleece-lined bloomers, one pair of black woollen stockings, a navy blue dress and clean towels. We took this with us and all headed for the laundry room. Inside there were eight galvanized tubs ready for use. These tubs were all filled by hand and had to be emptied the same way. We bathed two to a tub. Sometimes it got so steamed up that we could not see who our partners were. Our hair was washed by the bigger girls. Following this a jug of cold water was poured over us. This was to shrink

Bath night in the laundry room.

George Hunter

our pores so that we would not catch cold, we were politely told.

Saturday was the most pleasant day of the week. We did all our housework in the morning — sweeping and dusting and tidying our dorms. After lunch, if we had parents in town, we could go home for the afternoon. I sometimes went home with my good friend who was called Peanuts because of her size. Her house was right in Aklavik. Then we went out to the Hudson's Bay store or to visit our other friends. Sometimes we just sat at home enjoying the family atmosphere. After the crowded school life it felt good to be by ourselves for a while. Her mother would remind us that it was almost time to leave and we would collect some dried meat, bannock, butter, and sweets to take back to school with us.

Once a week, usually on Sunday, we were given seven candies by our supervisor. We were not allowed to eat them all at once. Instead we put them in a small box with our name on it and each night before bedtime we were allowed to have one candy. Sometimes we promised a friend a candy in return for a favour, and so that day we would have to go without.

Something else that we had each day was cod-liver oil, and it sure didn't taste good. It came in five-gallon cans on the boat during the summer. Before it was dished out it was poured into a two-pound can which our supervisor held. We would file past her each morning for a tablespoon and then dash to the toilet to spit it out. When our supervisor caught on to this we had to stay and open our mouths to show that we had swallowed the horrid stuff. I guess that was why we were so healthy. But by the time the five-gallon can was empty it was so rancid you could smell it a mile away. I have never taken cod-liver oil since.

CHAPTER SIX

Christmas

IT WAS MY FIRST CHRISTMAS at school. Christmas, up until this time, had been a season for feasts and games. In school things were different. I was told that we would sing carols for our parents, and have a pageant, whatever that was. I soon found out that it had something to do with acting out parts. My first part in a pageant was one of the three wise men. I had heard of the wise men before. They were the ones who brought gifts to the baby Jesus. What strange gifts — gold, frankincense and myrrh! Our gifts to anyone we loved had always been clothing and food.

School work was forgotten and we were coached in our parts. Then my friends began to talk about Santa Claus.

"What is a Santa Claus?" I asked.

"Oh, just wait and see," they replied.

The pageant was to be held on Christmas Eve, and the stage was set up in one of the classrooms.

All day long an air of mystery prevailed. I kept asking Peanuts what was going on.

"Be patient," she said. "Just wait and see."

After supper we put on our costumes. By seven o'clock the town people started to come in. My stomach did flip-flops. I was still not sure of what we were all doing. At eight o'clock our costumes were straightened for the last time. Mary and Joseph went out onto the stage and the Baby Jesus, lying in a manger, was placed beside them. The curtain was drawn back. I had never seen so many people in all my life.

The choir began singing "We Three Kings of Orient Are." That was my cue. For one awful minute I could not get my feet to move. Finally someone pushed me out on stage. I bowed towards the manger, stepped back behind Joseph and my part was finished. Then, horror of horrors, I got the giggles. The choir kept on singing. Our director, just off stage behind the curtain, gave me dirty looks and that sobered me up. Several other short plays were acted out and then we all went back on stage for the last carol. The audience stood up and clapped. Then the teachers helped us to take off our costumes and we went out to join the visitors for hot chocolate and doughnuts.

When we went out of the classroom I saw a big evergreen tree sitting in the hall, and I thought how strange the people were around here to bring a tree into the house. I decided not to ask any questions about it. I knew what the answer would be. "Be patient. Wait and see."

Most of the other children had parents at the pageant, but not me. I talked to Peanuts' family and others I knew and then it was time for bed. I crawled in, tired but happy.

Now what was happening? I was given one stocking and I held it up, wondering where the other one was. I asked Peanuts a final question.

"Where is my other stocking? I only have one side."

Peanuts told me to come on with her and led me to the towel rack in the washroom.

"Hang it up there," she said.

Now I knew that everyone was crazy. Oh well, if they thought that by morning the other side would be there, who was I to question it? It seemed that I was hardly asleep when I heard a voice calling me.

"Alice, Alice. Wake up."

It was dawn and Peanuts was standing over me. There must be a fire, I thought. I looked around but no one had a parka on. She took me by the hand and we pushed through a crowd of girls to the washroom. She pointed to my stocking. Hey, it was filled up with something! We went back to our rooms and emptied our stockings on our beds. There was a necklace, a handkerchief, soap, toothpaste, an orange and candy.

"Hey, Connie. Who filled up our stockings?"

She was so busy she did not even look up.

"Betty, who filled our stockings?"

"Santa Claus. He came down the chimney while we were asleep."

There was that name again. He must be awfully small, I thought, and safe from fire and heat to slide down the chimney.

Then the trading started.

"I will trade you my brooch and candy for your necklace."

"No, but I will trade your necklace for my ring."

If we were good at bargaining, we came away with more than we started with. If we weren't good at it, too bad.

Then it was time to get dressed and go down to breakfast. On my way down the stairs, I stopped. There, in front of my eyes, was the most

glorious tree I had ever seen. It was the same
tree that had been in the hall the night before,
but now it was transformed. It had so many toys
and so much tinsel on it that I could hardly see
any of the green needles. Dolls, trucks, books,
games and everything I could imagine were
hanging from it.

Breakfast was another surprise. Instead of porridge and molasses, there was juice, cornflakes,
coffee and a roll. I was beginning to think that
there was a lot to Christmas after all.

Prayers took a long time that morning. We
knew exactly when to say "Amen," and we said
it quickly before the boys' supervisor, Mr.
Ellwyn, could change his mind. Then we sat down
to tackle breakfast. After we had eaten we played
in the playroom until the girls on kitchen and
dining-room duty had washed the dishes and
cleaned the rooms.

Finally they joined us, and the supervisor came
in and told us to line up. We marched out into
the hall and there was my mysterious Santa Claus
at last. He was not small as I had imagined. He
was huge, and he wore a red suit and had a long
white beard. He started to call out names and
give away toys. He called my name and I went
to him and received a doll. My brother, I saw,

had a gun set. He seemed to be just as bewildered as I was. I went over to him and asked him if he was happy.

"Yes," he said.

He felt shy in front of the other boys because of my attention, so I left him. But at least I knew he was happy. We went back to the playroom and the others started to trade their gifts. Not me, I was going to keep my doll.

One of the girls told me that after lunch we could go home for the afternoon and for every afternoon that week, if our parents were in Akla-vik. My father did not come in for Christmas that year. I wondered where he was. I missed him. But each day was too exciting to miss him for long. The Christmas holidays passed and it was soon time for us to go back to our lessons.

CHAPTER SEVEN

Winter Studies

M Y TEACHER'S NAME was Miss A. Farrow and after Christmas her job was much easier for we were all able to speak fairly well in English. I was luckier than some of my girl friends, because I had learned English from my father. We had not been allowed to speak our native tongue since coming to school and it was hard on some of my friends. If we were caught speaking in Eskimo we were punished. This was a frustrating but effective system.

I really did not mind reading and writing but I sure did not like arithmetic. Some of the subjects we read about puzzled me. Dogs I already knew about, and cats. I had seen my first horse, but what were sheep and cows and pigs? Chickens looked something like ptarmigan and the eggs were good to eat. We learned a nursery rhyme:

Humpty Dumpty sat on a wall
Humpty Dumpty had a great fall
All the king's horses and all the king's men

Couldn't put Humpty Dumpty together again.

According to the picture book Humpty Dumpty was an egg, so how could he be dressed and sitting on a wall? I asked Miss Farrow about this and did not seem to get any answers. A rhyme that puzzled me even more was:

Hey diddle diddle, the cat and the fiddle
The cow jumped over the moon
The little dog laughed to see such sport
And the dish ran away with the spoon

Now, I knew cats could not play fiddles. I did not know whether cows could jump over the moon or not, but I was sure that dishes could not run and certainly not with spoons. I worried about my teacher sometimes. She did not seem to know the difference between what creatures could and could not do.

Each year, as my reading got better, I found that books held a vast store of information and could take me away to distant times and places. I learned that Ottawa was our capital city in Canada. That was where our Prime Minister lived. He was the one who told everyone else how to live. Besides Canada there were different countries with different kinds of people. England was the country where my teacher used to live. This was hard to feature but I told myself never

Alice, wearing the parka her mother made for her, stands in the doorway of a tent in the schoolyard.   Anglican Church of Canada Archives

mind; there were all my tomorrows ahead to learn something new.

Wintertime in the Mackenzie was cold and dark, quite depressing sometimes, especially from the end of November on when the sun no longer came up. Mid-day brought a little twilight and our walks were much shorter now, because of the cold weather. We went just around to The Bay store, about half a mile away, and back. My winter clothing was not as warm as my fur clothes used to be. My parka, mitts and mukluks were made from blanket cloth, covered with blue denim, and the wind blew right through them. Only the soles of my boots were made of skin — moose-hide. The only birds we saw on our walks were the ravens rooting in the garbage for food, and the occasional whiskey jack. On some nights the moon was full and shining; it transformed our dark world into a land of shimmering brightness. Looking out our dormitory window we could see the snow-covered trees and houses much better than we could during the day.

Quite frequently in the cold months we would wake up in the night shivering with cold and head for the hot-air radiator. Some nights I was lucky because no one else was up and I could have the radiator to myself for a while. I let the hot air billow out my nightgown and warm my body with heat. Then more girls woke up cold and I got off and sat on the floor, with just my feet on the radiator. Soon there would be ten or twelve girls shoving each other for a place on the radiator. Then I would crawl back into bed.

Fire drills were a nightmare for us all. We never

knew when they would be called. Sometimes they were a week apart; other times three or four weeks would go by before we would hear the alarm. Each evening, before bedtime, we collected our parkas, mitts, and mukluks from the playroom and took them up and laid them at the foot of our beds. Then as we undressed we placed our dresses, stockings, bloomers and longjohns on top of our outer clothing. Most of the time we were careless and did not bother. When the alarm went off in the middle of the night we had only three minutes to dress and that was just enough time to put on our parkas, boots, and mittens. In the fall and spring drills were not bad, but in the winter it was cold. We lined up in front of the fire-escape window, which was located in our dorm, and waited for the signal. We were to start sliding down the chute every three seconds. Our supervisor, Miss Neville, counted — one, two, three — and the first girl started off. There was a small platform attached to the window with a slide leading to the ground floor below. Often one girl would stand on the platform and look down and be scared. She would hesitate for a second and that would throw the rest of us off. Miss Neville was not able to see what was happening at the bottom and would still keep sending girls on down. Soon we had a tangle of bodies in the snow below. After one of these drills we came back in with our teeth chattering. It would be a while before we went back to sleep and the next day it was a chore to stay awake in classes.

As we grew older we helped in the kitchen, dining-room, and staff dining-room. We were taught the use of the washing machine and the mangle. We worked one day a week at each chore. I hated to work in the dining-room. We had to wash all the dishes by hand. When we worked in the staff dining-room we learned the correct way to set tables and serve the meals. I did not mind this job; we ate the same meals as the staff. Once a week, in the evenings, we helped to punch down the bread dough. Before breakfast we put this dough into breadpans, ready to bake.

The days were getting longer now that January was almost over. The sun started peeking up, just a sliver at first, but each day it got a little stronger and I was glad that the long darkness had ended. Now our afternoon walks were through the bush. This was to allow us to snare rabbits which we sold to the school for 25 cents each. If we were successful we could make quite a bit of pocket money. On Saturdays our walks were much longer and we took along a picnic. We would walk about three miles, stop, build a roaring fire and huddle around it trying to warm ourselves. The hot tea always tasted good and so did the wieners and buns that we toasted over the fire. After eating, we relaxed and sang camp-fire songs around the fire.

Sometimes we played hookey on our walks through the settlement. If our supervisor needed something from The Bay store and went in to buy it, we would run back to the school. If we were caught at this we would be sent to the principal's office, and sometimes we got the strap. At recess or on days we did not go for walks, we made our own entertainment. We had a swing in the yard and a slide made out of snow and ice. Our sleds were pieces of heavy cardboard that we soaked in water and left out to freeze overnight so they would go faster and farther down the slide. Even though we liked the slide we were usually glad to go back into the warm school.

CHAPTER EIGHT

Spring

THE COMING OF SPRING was looked forward to by everyone. From March 15 until June 15 was the ratting season in the Mackenzie Delta. During this time of year the trappers made the bulk of their money. If the market was good and the muskrats were plentiful life would be just that much easier during the coming year. Some of the boys and girls left school at this time to help their parents. Most of their families lived in the bush beside good muskrat lakes and channels. Even in school we were given two traps each and taught how to use them. So, in the spring our walks included lakes which had muskrat houses. The pelts we sold to the Hudson's Bay store and the meat was roasted for us to eat at the school.

In the spring, the Mackenzie Delta was beautiful. It was a land of muskeg, rivers, lakes and trees. It had mountains and hills on some parts of it. *Amauligaqs* — the snowbirds — came first in the spring. It was a joy to see them after a season with few birds. It signalled that spring was on the way. The ptarmigan fed on the pussy-willow buds and we children gathered tender young willow leaves to eat. We stripped the bark off the branches and sucked them; the juice tasted sweet and good. During our spring walks we looked for sorrel, which tasted like rhubarb. The liquorice plant, which we called *mussu*, was gathered, washed, and eaten raw. Sometimes we dug in the ground and found edible roots, shaped like almonds, which we called truffles.

Soon the land was filled with birds. Mallards and other ducks paired off to nest by our rivers and lakes. Most of the geese flew on to the coast to mate and bring up their young on the tundra. By mid-July whistling swans, with one or two downy cygnets, would be paddling proudly up and down the channels of the Mackenzie, as if to say "Look what beautiful children we have." Terns, gulls and skuas went to Gull Island near Kiklavik Bay to have their young. If we went anywhere near the island we would be scolded and attacked. Eider ducks went farther north, but some of the loons stayed in the Mackenzie. If we happened to come across one of their nests

we did not stop to examine the eggs. We would
have been dive-bombed. Loons were very fierce
in the protection of their young. Young ptarmigan
were fluffy and round but very fast on their feet,
especially when being chased by a kid who
wanted them for pets. Cranes did their mating
dance before pairing off. If we saw one feeding
on the ground, we would sing to it and it would
flap its wings and jump up and down, doing its
dance for us.

Young Canada geese break out of their shells.

Songbirds came in thousands. Horned larks
woke us up with their glad morning songs. Robins
were busy gathering twigs and bright pieces of
cloth to build their nests. There was a weird bird,
probably the Common Snipe, that flew up in the
sky until we could see it no more. Then with
its wings against its body, it plunged towards the
ground, singing, until we thought it was going
to crash. At the last minute it would unfold its
wings to fly up and begin all over. We called
it the rain bird, because after one of these displays
it always rained. There were waders of all kinds;
turnstones and plovers that fooled us with their
broken-wing trick; many curlews and whimbrels
and birds of prey: hawks, owls and falcons.

The countryside was soon bright with colour.
Pink fireweed sprang up everywhere. The marshy
ponds were covered with yellow marsh mari-
golds. Certain small streams, rippling through the
bush, had watercress along their banks. We gathered this to eat instead of mussu, whose root was
stringy and tough by the time the purple vetch
flowers came out. In the settlement dandelions,
yellow buttercups, and green grass covered the
ground around the houses and sidewalks. They
made a scene that had been dreary and dirty,
pleasant to look upon. The green leaves against

the white bark of the birch trees and the light green tips of the spruce branches made our after-school walks a pleasure.

On the tundra the delicate white pink of the blueberry blossom and the white flowers, edged with deep red, of the cranberry plant, told us where there would be an abundance of berries for later picking — unless a late frost came to kill them while in blossom. The bells of the arctic heather showed white among the green leaves of the Labrador tea and made a delightful scent when we walked on them. We watched for the star-shaped flower of the delicious akpik berry along the lakes and valleys of the tundra and noted where they grew the thickest; we would be back later in the summer to pick them.

Midway through June the ice on the rivers and lakes started to melt along the shore. Every year the Mackenzie River overflowed its banks. Once it flooded past our school and the people, using canoes, paddled from one house to the other. Empty 45-gallon fuel drums were set out to mark the boundary of the breakup. Pool tickets, with the hour, minute and second of the ice breakup, were sold. The holder of the ticket closest to the actual time of breakup won a considerable amount of money.

The 'Distributor' takes school children for a ride at Fort Resolution.

HBC

Shortly after the river was clear of ice we watched for the paddle-wheeler, the *Distributor*, to arrive from the south. There was another pool on the first sighting of this boat rounding the bend in the river. It carried mostly fresh fruit and vegetables for the settlements along the river. The people were hungry for the taste of apples, oranges, potatoes, onions and eggs, after eating

canned or dried ones all winter. Before leaving
to go back up river the captain took the children
from both schools for a boat-ride.

A few days later other boats arrived with food
supplies and dry goods for the Hudson's Bay and
for Mr. H. E. Peffer who was a free trader, and
owned a store and a hotel in Aklavik. Mail orders
from catalogues, sent out to be filled the past
winter, also arrived on these boats. When we
opened the crates and parcels we found that a
lot of things had been substituted. Notes were
attached from Eaton's and Simpson's saying that
the items enclosed were of better make or
material and more expensive than the original
order; if goods were not satisfactory they could
be returned and the money would be cheerfully
refunded. No one ever sent back an order — the
article would have taken until the following year
to return. No liquor was brought up on these
boats so far as I knew except, perhaps, a few
cases the white people had ordered.

CHAPTER NINE

The School in Summer

M Y BROTHER and I stayed at school during the summer holidays for three years,
because our father was not able to come to Aklavik
for us. Ordinarily I would be upset when the
last two weeks in June came. That was the time
to houseclean the school for the holidays and
then my girl friends would pack their belongings
to go home to their parents. I had to stay in the
school all summer, for there was nowhere else
to go. It was pathetic to have only a few of us
rattling around inside a big building that was
made to house hundreds of children. Our voices
carried from room to room when we talked and
our footsteps echoed through the hallways. It felt
creepy at night trying to go to sleep with a room
full of empty beds for company. The teachers
who could not afford to go home to England every
year stayed with us and they were just as lonesome as we were. They tried to make our summer
pass as pleasantly as possible by taking us on

51

camping trips and picnics during those lonely weeks.

Each spring the Reverend Shepherd would plant a vegetable garden behind his house — carrots, onions, radishes and potatoes — but they did not grow very big. We did not help matters any because the minute they were big enough to eat we would snitch them. He put a chicken-wire fence around the garden, but we soon learned to pull it up and crawl on our stomachs to reach the vegetables. One afternoon Connie was lying under the fence digging for baby pota-toes, while we held up the wire. The next thing we knew Reverend Shepherd was standing beside us. No one had noticed him coming. He gave her a whack across the bottom and pulled her out. When Connie looked up and saw who was pull-ing her, she started to cry. For this trick we were all put to work, weeding and hoeing, for the rest of the afternoon. The next afternoon we were still working off our debt to him when we noticed the sky growing dark and the huskies started to howl. We huddled together, crying with fright, thinking that it was the end of the world. Rever-end Shepherd came over to us and explained that the moon was coming between the earth and the sun and cutting off the light. It was called an

The Reverend H. S. Shepherd, seated aboard the mission launch at Aklavik.

Anglican Church of Canada Archives

eclipse of the sun, he told us. We felt much better then, as we watched the sun starting to emerge again and the daylight return to normal.

After three summers at the school I finally went home. Grandfather Okalisok and grandma Kakotok, my mother's parents, came into the settlement and my brother and I were to go home with them. After lunch, we were packed and ready. I glanced out of the window and I saw my grandparents sitting in the yard waiting for the bell to ring at one o'clock. Then they would come in to get us. Oh no! There was my grandfather taking his parka off and he did not even have a shirt on under it. I hoped that he would put it back on again. Feeling a bit uneasy, I heard the bell ring and in they came to take us home. With a feeling of relief, I saw that my grandfather had donned his parka before coming in. We went to their tent which was pitched below the school.

Oh! It certainly was good to be home again. At that time of the year the sun shone all night and I did not have to go to bed, unless I felt like it. My grandmother told us that our father had remarried. He would be coming into Aklavik with his new family and we would be going to stay with them. After a few days my dad came to fetch us.

"We have a new home," he said. "You must say good-bye to your grandparents and come and meet your new ones." I was glad to see my father again but felt sad, having to say goodbye to grandpa Okalisok and grandma Kakotok and the rest of my mother's family.

As we crossed the river by canoe to my father's tent, I felt a bit worried about meeting this new family. We were introduced to Unalena, his wife; Susie and Amos Tuma, her parents; and all kinds of aunts and uncles who were waiting to see what sort of children my father was bringing into the family. I met everyone and then I asked if I could go back to my granny's now. My father said "No, this is your home and these are your grand-parents." It would be a few years before I stayed with my mother's people again. Grandma Susie Tuma did not feel that it was right for someone else to look after me now that I was part of her family.

In Aklavik Dominion Day was a big event. The day before July 1, the women in the village would go from door to door collecting food for the feast that would be held in the evening after the sports were over. They got fish and meat, bannock, bread, canned fruit, pies, cakes, candy, and cooked meats.

The next day we had all kinds of races. There was javelin-throwing and pole-vaulting and eating contests. Competition between the whites, Indians and Eskimos was keen. Between the Anglican and Roman Catholic children there was rivalry too. We worked hard to see who could collect the most ribbons for our schools. Tug-of-war and baseball games rounded out the after-noon. By now, some of us had a few bruises and skinned knees.

Finally a tarpaulin was laid on the ground and

food was set in the middle of it and everyone started eating. I found my dad. He saw the red ribbon I was wearing and asked what I got that for.

"Oh, for a doughnut-eating contest," I replied.

"I suppose you are not hungry now?"

I said that I was starved. It had been only one doughnut tied on a string, and I had to stand under it with my hands tied back behind my back. I finished my doughnut first before the others and won the ribbon. After we finished eating everyone helped to clean up the grounds and pick up the remains of the food. This was distributed among the old folks.

There was a dance at Peffer's Hall that night and my dad promised to take me to it. When we were there he taught me the waltz and the two-step. I felt proud to be dancing with him. At eleven-thirty my grandmother Susie said that there was an Eskimo dance that they would like to go to, so we went back across the river to our camp where these dances were being held. It was not as exciting as the dance at Peffer's Hall.

CHAPTER TEN

Grandmother Susie

M Y GRANDMOTHER Susie was the head of our household. She was also a *suptakti* — an Eskimo doctor, and a very good one. She was a spry little woman with blue tattoo marks on her chin and black and gray hair that hung to her shoulders. She kept a close watch over her household, but she dropped everything if a sick person was brought to our house, or sent for her to come to them. Her services were always in demand in times of illness or when a baby was being born.

For a severe headache my grandmother would make a small cut on the crown of the head to bleed the patient. If the problem was internal she would rub the tummy with her small hands until she knew what was wrong and then she would put it right again. For snow-blindness she made a cut in the right temple or put boiled leaves in a cloth which she then laid on the eyes to soothe them. For a serious attack of pain in the area of the liver — which today we would call a gall-bladder attack — she would set coal oil on fire and allow it to burn until most of it had evaporated and turned brown. Then she would rub the tender area, gently massaging in the brown stuff until the gall stones were moved away from the bile duct. She used chewing tobacco for toothache and she made us swallow tobacco juice for chest pains and coughing.

My grandmother helped many people. If I began to name all those whom she treated, I would be putting down half the people in the Delta.

We did not live in snow-houses in the Mackenzie Delta. We lived during the cold months in a house that had been built up from drift logs over a number of years. When the ice broke up in the spring it was the job of the children to watch for logs in the floating ice. When we saw one, the men would go out after it in a canoe.

The house was about twenty-six feet wide and twenty feet deep — all one room with an addition on it for a married aunt and her husband, and a porch where we stored harnesses and firewood and cooked food for the dogs. Inside, the beds were curtained off. My parents had their bed in one corner and my grandparents were in the opposite corner. In between were three beds for the girls, made of lumber and canvas, with mattresses and comforters stuffed with duck and goose feathers. The boys slept in eiderdown sleeping-bags on caribou skins on the floor.

We had two stoves. One was a 45-gallon oil drum which we filled with green logs and lit just before bedtime. The other was our cook-stove. My grandmother always kept a can of Lysol steaming on the back of the stove. It made the house smell clean, she said, and it kept germs away.

My grandmother had a thing about cleanliness. On Saturdays we cleaned the house right through. The work began Friday night when we sorted the dirty clothes and filled all the boilers and tubs with ice that melted and heated while we were asleep. Then in the morning, right after breakfast, we girls got busy with wash-tubs and scrub-boards and lots of Sunlight soap. We put the bedding out on the line to air and in the afternoon we scrubbed the rough lumber floor with lye and water until my grandmother was satisfied that it was white enough.

Every night before we went to bed we swept the house in case we had travellers come in during the night. We did not ordinarily use the table for eating because there were too many of us. Instead we spread an oilcloth on the floor and ate sitting around it. If a white trapper came by on his way to his trap-line he ate his breakfast on the table under the window.

In the summer we lived in tents. Each family had its own. In my day the tents were canvas, but long ago my great-grandparents made tents of caribou skins and willow branches. I saw them build these tents. The skins were scraped until there was no hair on them, and then they were sewn together. Quite a lot of light came in through the skins.

Not many Eskimo women held the position of head of the house as my grandmother Susie did. She administered the discipline, supervised the family, and ruled with an iron hand. During my sewing lessons she had me sit in front of her where she could look down on my sewing and see how I was doing. I am afraid I gave her a lot of problems. I did not know how to hold the needle or scraper properly or how to make thread from the sinew of caribou. In fact I was quite dumb, she thought. Any ten-year-old girl should have known how to do these things. So my lessons were longer than anyone else's. First

I had to learn to scrape skins — they had to be soft enough for her to be able to scrunch up in her hand; that took days of scraping and rubbing. Then I had to learn to cut out mukluks and parkas, and to sew them. My stitches had to be so small that she could not see them from where she sat and that took some doing. If I made a mistake or took too big a stitch her finger, with a thimble attached, came down on top of my skull with a knock and I was told to take the whole thing apart and start over again, no matter how close the garment was to completion. It really was frustrating, but I soon learned to do things well the first time so that I would not have to do them over again and again.

When the sewing lessons were over I had to sit and pluck gray hairs from her head. This was to keep my fingers limbered up. I was not allowed to use tweezers for this job and she kept track of only the very short ones that I had managed to pull out. When she was satisfied that I had pulled enough out she released me from this chore. While I was doing this she would tell me Eskimo stories and so I really did not mind my job. I loved to listen to the folk tales. I wish that I had paid more attention to all these stories, now that she is gone — but at that time I was still

Grandfather Amos Tuma.

going to boarding school and I thought I knew so much better. I did not think that life would ever change and thought that I had all the time in the world to learn about the things that belonged to my people, the Inuit.

My grandmother was most bull-headed when she wanted to be. No one dared oppose her when she decided on the course of action to take next. All of us, including her married sons and daughters who lived with her, had a healthy respect for her temper. She was a remarkable woman and kept the family together until her death.

My grandfather, on the other hand, was a quiet and soft-spoken gentleman. He did not need to scold us to make us do our work. He just made a suggestion and we did it gladly. When my grandmother was especially hard on me he quietly told her that I was doing fine for a girl who had no knowledge of the many things she expected of me. He was kind and considerate and acted as a buffer between her and the rest of the family. He never openly opposed her decisions, but sometimes he suggested doing things in a different way and made her believe that it was her idea in the first place.

CHAPTER ELEVEN

Whaling Camp

THAT SUMMER in the second week of July grandmother decided it was time to be on our way to the whaling camp. My father took the schooner over to the Hudson's Bay store to load up with provisions for the trip down to Whitefish Station on the coast of the Beaufort Sea. By the time he was back we had the tents down and all the household things packed and ready for loading. The women and children carried the bags and boxes on board while the men loaded the 45-gallon drums which would be used for storing the whale blubber and dried meat.

Then came the hardest job. Between all the hunters in our family there were about forty dogs that had to be loaded on board. I loathed this task, mainly because I was scared to death of the dogs and they sensed this. Unfortunately the dog I picked to lead on board first hated to walk the plank. We were halfway up, and I was feeling proud of myself for not being in a panic, when

Whaling schooners beached on the shore at Aklavik. The Tuma house was across the river.   HBC

this one dog decided he did not want to go on the boat after all. Without warning he turned around and headed back to shore. The gangplank was narrow and there was not enough room for both of us side by side. If I had been a little bigger, like the others, I would have been able to pick him up and head him back on board. But I was small and I found myself shoved off the plank into the muddy river below. When I was being helped onto shore someone shouted, "Alice, did you want a bath so badly you could not wait to heat the water for your tub?"

My grandmother, who was supervising the loading, shouted in Eskimo "Anisalouk, you have brought me a *doditchiak* (grandchild) who is *beyaptangga* (clumsy)." I was embarrassed for both myself and my dad.

Then when I tied up the dogs, I found that I had put two dogs that hated each other close together and I was bitten on the thumb. That was the last straw. Crying with frustration and pain I ran down below and no amount of coaxing would make me come up on the deck until the dogs were all on board and we were underway.

It was a beautiful evening as we pushed off and headed down the Mackenzie River bound for the coast. I soon forgot my troubles and helped to fix up the sleeping quarters and prepare the first meal on board. The oilcloth was laid on deck and we had a relay line passing food from the kitchen below. While we were eating we children talked about the fun we would have on the coast. I looked at the shoreline and made believe that the first row of spruce trees was running to keep up with us, and that the back row was urging them to catch us. We turned off into one of the many channels; the water was clear and calm, like a mirror reflecting trees, banks and sky. Clumps of reddish-pink fireweed

and yellow buttercups were everywhere and we
could smell the faint scent of wild roses and the
strong earthy smell of the forest. As I sat on deck
that evening I felt content and happy. Later I went
down to bed and fell asleep listening to the
sounds of the schooner swishing through the
water.

When I woke the next morning I went on deck
and found that we were just passing John Kivak's
place. He was a well-known trapper in the Delta
who lived on the east branch of the Mackenzie
River. Reindeer Station was not far off. We would
stop there for a day to feed and water the dogs.
The reindeer had been herded into Canada from
Alaska, as a government plan to provide food
during famine years. A group of Laplanders made
the long journey across nearly 2,000 miles from
Alaska to the reindeer reserve east of the
Mackenzie River. It took them five years of hard
work — from Christmas 1929 until February 1935
— before they settled down at Reindeer Station
and began to teach our people how to look after
the reindeer herd. I grew up with Ellen Palk who
later became Mrs. Otto Binder. Her family was
one of the original families who brought the herd
into Canada.

Reindeer Station was the main depot for the

Reindeer Station.   H B C

reindeer herd and the families who tended them. There were seven log cabins, four frame houses for the white families and The Bay store that had a house attached for the clerk and various warehouses. By the time we got there the herders had gone down to Kiklavik Bay with the herd for the summer. The grounds around the cabins were covered with fireweed and bumble bees were busy feeding on the flowers. We went ashore to climb up Station Hill for a bit of exercise and as we waded through the flowers my aunt Olga, who was walking behind me, said, "A bee just flew up under your parka cover." I started to scream and shake my cover, trying to dislodge it. I had a phobia about bees and bugs and I could not control my screaming. Finally my aunt came to my rescue, lifted up my parka cover and released the trapped bee. We continued on our walk and by the time we reached the top of the hill I had stopped shaking. Looking down, I saw the lakes and rivers of the Mackenzie Delta stretched out before me. Close by in a patch of stunted willows, I could hear the ptarmigan call "Go back, go back, cok, cok", and siksik, the ground squirrel, scolded us for disturbing him. The spruce trees were all one-sided, shaped by the strong prevailing north winds. There were small ponds with ducks on them, and birds flitting from tree to tree. Arctic heather, blueberry, cranberry, and Labrador tea bushes grew in clumps along with the caribou moss and other low tundra plants. As we started back down towards the boat I felt a bit leery about going through the fireweed but I arrived at the boat without further mishap.

The next morning we were underway again. We would not stop until we arrived at Lucas Point where some other families had already camped.

We unloaded the dogs, pitched our tents, and the men set out nets for fresh fish. Soon we had whitefish boiling in a big kettle on a tripod over an open fire. Bannock was baking over hot coals and that, with lots of tea, was our supper. Afterwards our dishes were washed in the river and our housework was done for the day. No scrubbing of floors or sweeping; we just had to gather a few bits of driftwood for the cooking fires. We stayed a few days and then started on the last lap of the journey.

As we got closer to the coast the landscape started to change. The trees got fewer and smaller. Soon there were no trees, just gently rolling hills, gravel beaches, and clear blue water. The muddy waters of the Mackenzie River were left behind and we sailed along on the clear, clean-smelling sea.

Our destination, Whitefish Station, was about twenty miles from Tuktoyaktuk on the Beaufort Sea. For many years my people had gone there every summer for whaling. For me, the whaling camp had only happy memories. There was not a tree to hamper the vision of sea and sky and land. On a clear day we could see the mirage of Tuktoyaktuk hanging upside down in the sky and Kiklavik Bay, ten miles across the ocean.

At the Whitefish whaling camp.

Collection: Alice French

While we were living on the coast we depend-
ed on the sea for our food and we had to be very
careful not to anger the sea spirit. This meant
that we could not work on the skins of land
animals. There was rivalry between the sea and
land spirits in providing man with his livelihood.
Should we be so foolish as to forget this rule,
the sea spirit would cause storms to keep us from
going out to hunt on the sea. She might also lead
all the sea creatures away in her jealousy.

Our whaling trip included all my grandfather's
family. There were my uncles Michael, Harry,
Colin, and Donald, and my aunts Olga, Agnes,

and Mary. My grandma's married sister and husband were with us, and then there was our own family of six. In all we had five tents. The whaling camp, as a whole, was made up of some thirty to forty families. A freshwater creek flowed into the sea and made a good harbour for our boats.

Once we had settled in, my grandfather went up the hills with his binoculars, and soon sighted some whales. The men launched the boats and headed out to sea. They could be gone a few hours, or all night, so we supplied the boat with enough food to last for two days. When a boat returned we looked at the mast to see how many banners were flying. Our boat had two on the mast when it came in. This meant that they had two whales. Everyone rushed to the beach to help pull the white whales to shore. The children, with their jack-knives and small ulus, cut bits of muktuk off the tail flipper and ate it raw. Then the women began to work and within an hour the whale was just a skeleton. The meat was sliced into big slabs and hung up on the racks to dry. The blubber was stripped off the hide, sliced into narrow strips and stored in the 45-gallon drums we brought with us. The first layer of the hide was made into muktuk. It was cut into nine-by-nine-inch squares, hung on racks in bunches of

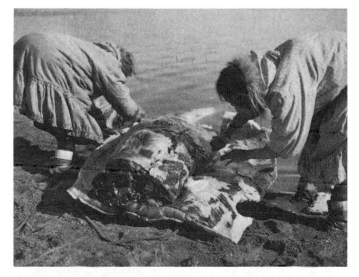

Carving up a white whale. The woman on the right carries a baby under her parka.   H B C

A float made from the whale's stomach is inflated to mark the position of a harpooned whale.   H B C

ten and dried for two to three days. Then it was
cooked and put into the same barrel as the blubber. This preserved it for eating through the
winter months. The middle layer of the hide,
called ganek, was stretched, dried, and used for
shoe leather.

Grandfather was kept busy making ulus and
sharpening them. My grandmother's job was to
teach us the art of cutting up the whale and
making use of every bit of it. She taught us how
to make containers from the stomach, but first
we had to practice separating the layers of skin
on the throat. Until we could do this without
putting a hole in the skin, we were not allowed
to start the more serious task of container making.
There were three layers to the stomach and it
took two hours to take them apart. Only the
middle layer was used. This was blown up and
dried for use as a container for whale oil, dried
meat, dried fish and bits of muktuk for the winter.
The containers were also used for storing blueberries and cranberries and for floats to mark
the position of a harpooned whale.

At the whaling camp the girls learned to make
waterproof boots. The top part was made of
canvas or of seal skin; the sole of the boot was
made from whaleskin, crimped with the teeth.

I was not good at this, much to my grandmother's dismay. As a result my value as a wife went down. Almost all our clothing was made by hand, so it was important to be good at all these things.

Whaling camp was a place where the young people had fun. The boys and girls did not pair off by themselves, but they were allowed to go with a crowd to dances and picnics. During the day we worked hard, but the evenings were ours to spend as we pleased. One day we arranged to go with others to pick salmonberries which grew in abundance along a lake about three miles inland. Since I and a couple of single aunts would be with a group, my grandmother gave us permission to go. While we were packing a lunch she told us not to *deeduk* (fool around). "I know there will be boys going, so behave yourselves," she warned, "or it will be the last time you girls go out, crowd or no crowd." At that time of year it was daylight all around the clock so we had all night to pick berries and have fun. When we were a quarter of a mile from the lake we saw the red-gold berries stretching as far as the eye could see. We raced to see who could fill up their container first. When every pot and pail was full we had our picnic lunch beside the lake.

It did not matter when we came home to bed

as long as we woke up the minute our grandmother called us. So we played baseball, hide-
and-seek and *mara mara* (prisoner's base) out on
the tundra. Most evenings there were dances but
they were mostly Eskimo dances. I tried hard to
learn drum dancing but I was not graceful
enough. My arms and feet refused to relax and
flow gracefully. Once a week or so we had a
fiddler and a guitar player and we had square
dances.

Mid-August was reindeer round-up time in
Kiklavik, so we all went across the bay to visit
and help with the tagging and castration of the
deer. We were paid one carcass of meat per
family for this work. When we came back to
camp we dried the meat and stored it.

During all this time the grandmothers had been
busy matchmaking. Each one would tell the other
about the virtues of the boy or girl whose marriage they were arranging. The prospective bride
and groom had no say in the matter. Once the
women reached an agreement it was final and
binding.

That summer I lost an aunt but gained an uncle.
My aunt was a very strong-willed girl, but she
lost the battle to her mother — grandmother Susie.
My aunt had a boyfriend whom she loved, but

grandmother thought he was not as suitable as the man she had chosen to be her daughter's husband. Grandmother pointed out to her the plight of old maid so-and-so who had refused to comply with the wishes of her parents. This old maid had to set up her own house and depend on the charity of others for the rest of her life. As far as grandmother was concerned she had made her decision and the matter was closed.

In our family as soon as a girl reached the age of puberty she was guarded and chaperoned by the elders in her family until a suitable marriage could be arranged for her. This was to ensure that she did not have an illegitimate baby. Babies in themselves were nothing to be ashamed of. There was always someone to love and adopt them. However, a baby born outside of marriage brought shame to the family. The girl's parents were shamed for not caring enough to arrange a suitable marriage; the girl herself was shamed for not waiting for this arrangement to be made.

It had been a carefree and happy summer, but now it was the end of August and time to start back. We stopped along the way to pick blueberries and cranberries and slowly made our way back to Aklavik. Here I was dropped off at school, but my brother Danny, now seven, stayed with the family and never went to school again. The schooner, with my family, sailed on up the river to their winter camp.

CHAPTER TWELVE

A Missing Child

B y September most of us were back in school. I was glad to see some of my old friends back again — Betty, Peanuts and Connie among them. Some of the older girls had left school for good and there were a few new faces. We had our routine coal-oiling of the hair, our school uniforms were issued, and our personal clothing and identities were put away for another term. We became just the Anglican School kids once more.

In the second week of September we were told that next week-end we would be going up the mountains to pick blueberries and cranberries for the coming winter. We looked forward to these trips for we were still suffering from bouts of homesickness after the recent summer at home.

The Anglican boat, with a barge attached to the bow, would take us up river for this excursion. Two tents rigged up fore and aft on the barge would be our home for a while. Children aged ten and over, in groups of twenty-five, went berry picking. The little ones, and the others who did not go this time, would have their turn later. There were two other trips planned, and one all-day picnic for the younger group to go on. The boys, on the other hand, would go to pick up the cordwood along the river. This was cut and piled along the shore of the river by the men who worked for the school in the summer.

After breakfast, in an air of excitement, we loaded our provisions and sleeping gear. As we climbed on board we had a roll-call. Our names were ticked off on the list, which would be checked again before coming home. This way our teachers would know when the correct number of girls were all back on board. The weather was clear and calm as we pushed off, and the sun was shining. We hoped that it would stay that way for the week-end while we were up there on the mountain picking berries. As we chugged along up river, we talked about our holidays and what we did during the summer. Then one of the girls started a singsong and before we knew it, it was time for lunch. As we were eating we rounded the last bend in the river. We had reached our destination — the foothills of the Richardson Mountains.

We saw the Roman Catholic mission boat tied up on shore and on landing we were told that one of their girls was missing. She was a deaf and dumb child, and somehow she had wandered away from her group. They had been searching all morning for her. After unloading and tying up the barge on shore, our boat went back to Aklavik to report the missing child. We were organized into groups to help look for her. Our teachers told us to stay close together and to come back at dusk, if we had not found her by then. When we came back to the barge that evening we were informed that she had not yet been located. Searching the next morning we stayed close together and called out, "Peanuts, where are you?" "Here." "Don't go far." "O.K." It developed into another day of fruitless searching and as we went to bed that night we talked in hushed whispers about the terror the lost girl must be experiencing. We knew that there were bears out there, but most frightening of all would be the darkness at night. The fact that she was not able to hear us shouting and not able to call out to us made the search for her more disheartening.

She had been lost for four days when we went on board the boat Monday evening to head back home. We felt close to each other as we shared our sadness and despair over the lost girl. A search party from the settlement was to stay and help the Roman Catholic staff to continue the search for a few more days. At the end of the week, as we waited for news of how things were going, we were told that the search had been discontinued. She was presumed to have died of exposure. The nights would have been too cold for her to survive with just the sweater that she had on over her dress when she wandered away. Our service that Sunday included a prayer for her soul and for the Catholic Mission people in their sorrow.

By the middle of September we had picked enough berries to last us through the winter. These, with dried fruits and a few crates of apples and oranges for special occasions, would be our desserts. Our meat supplies would be taken care of by the fathers who were hunters. This was the contribution our parents made to help to pay for our schooling. The money to pay for the staff and the upkeep of the buildings, came from the collection plates of the churches down south. This was supplemented by the government to keep the school and hospital going.

The caribou herds had now migrated back into

*Supplies for the winter are brought in to All Saints' Anglican
Residential School.*
                                    Anglican Church of Canada Archives

the Richardson Mountains range after calving and
foraging in the lowlands during the summer
months. Near the end of October hunters with
their dog-teams arrived daily to buy supplies
from The Bay and Peffer's stores in preparation
for the annual caribou hunt on the mountains.
If they were lucky in locating the caribou herds
we would have lots of meat. This was supplemented by fish — coney, whitefish, and
crooked-backs — which the men had already
donated. Gill nets were taken up in the hills by
the caribou hunters to set out for the land-locked
char in the lakes. This fish averaged about one-

and-a-half pounds and was red-fleshed. We seldom cooked it. It was delicious eaten raw.

The women did not go along on these hunts, for the men hoped to fill up the sleds with their catch. Instead they snared rabbits to bring in to the schools during the Christmas holidays. Reindeer carcasses were donated by the government equally to each school from the herd at Reindeer Station.

In this way our meat supply was brought in each year. I remember that one year sacks of dried buffalo meat were sent down from the parks branch at Fort Smith. It was dry and stringy. We did not appreciate this donation much. Our warehouses were full of fish, and whole carcasses of reindeer and caribou hung on hooks on the ceiling. We had no refrigerating plant so towards the end of the school year our fish thawed and tasted a little high. We had a root cellar in the basement of the school where we stored sacks of carrots, cabbages, onions and potatoes sent from the gardens in the south. These, with dehydrated vegetables, took care of the vegetables for our meals.

School continued on in much the same manner as other years. I joined Girl Guides and our junior church auxiliary. Our project for the year 1941 was knitting for the soldiers. My contribution was a pair of socks. The articles were sent out the following summer by boat to Edmonton for distribution to various army camps. Our other project was to gather the foil wrappers from gum and candy and send them out at the same time. The war was not affecting us as much as the people outside. We were told some kinds of food and gas were rationed, but we did not have that here. The only difference it made to us up north was the black-out curfew each evening after dark.

That spring twenty of us were sent one by one to the All Saints' Anglican Hospital to have our tonsils out. Three days later we were back in school with sore throats that we did not have before going in. So passed the school year.

CHAPTER THIRTEEN

Banks Island

I WAS ELEVEN in June 1941, and it was the turn-
ing point in my life. When I was home for the
summer my father gave me the good news. I
would not be going back to school in the fall,
but would accompany my family to Banks Island.
They were going to try their luck trapping white
Arctic foxes. The price of fox pelts had been
steadily rising, while the muskrat furs, which they
had trapped last season, were falling in price.

We spent four weeks whaling at Whitefish
Station and then set out for Tuktoyaktuk. There
we stayed for two weeks to load up on provisions
and hunting and trapping equipment. Then we
went on to our destination, De Salis Bay on Banks
Island.

The day before leaving Tuktoyaktuk, my
young aunt Agnes and I were playing rock babies.
We packed rocks in our parkas and carried them
around on our backs pretending they were babies.
As I bent over to hike my six-pound rock further

up on my back, it came crashing down on the back of my head. It stunned me for a bit. I fell to my knees, stars bursting all over. Agnes saw me fall and asked if I were all right. I said that I was fine, except for a little headache and butterflies in my stomach. By the time we arrived home, I was feeling quite sick. The previous winter I had fallen from the top of the banister rail at school, when I was leaning over and talking to one of the girls downstairs. This fall knocked me out cold, and I spent a week in bed, feeling the same way that I felt now. By the time we reached Banks Island I was very sick. My grandmother nursed me the best she could. All September, October, and most of November I seemed to live in an unreal world where I caught occasional glimpses of Granny sitting at my bed-side.

Then my grandmother remembered the Bible story of Jesus washing the feet of his disciples. She did the same for me and prayed to the Lord to spare my life and let me wake up well and in my right mind. A few days later I woke up and asked where we were and what day it was. The last I could remember was the beginning of our journey and I knew that it would have taken a few days to reach our destination. Granny told me that I had been in bed for the last three

A porch of snow blocks shields the entrance to this tent. On Banks Island the blocks completely enclosed the tents of Alice's parents and grandparents.

L. A. Learmonth

months, and that she had quite given up on me. The one last hope had been to wash my feet and put my life in God's hands. She said that her faith and belief in the miracles He had performed was made stronger by my waking up clear-eyed and not babbling like a fool.

It did not seem possible that I had lain sick in bed for so long. Then I tried to stand up. My legs refused to hold up and my body looked like a skeleton. The first few times I was up out of bed I literally crawled around on my hands and knees like a baby. Each day I felt a bit stronger and by Christmas time I was well enough to join the family for meals in my grandparents' house.

Looking around our home I saw that what I thought was a log house was in fact a double tent, 14 feet by 20 feet, with snow blocks built up against the walls and roof. Our tent and the tent where my grandparents lived had a connecting porch where dog harnesses hung on the walls. This was where the dog food was cooked every day on primus stoves. At the far end a snow-house had been added for storing the staples and fresh meat.

The dogs, on long leashes, were tied to posts placed in a semi-circle ten yards from the entrance to our tents. They would warn us if a polar bear ever came close to the camp; their barking would discourage him from entering the porch.

By February I was well enough to help with the chores. The most pressing one was finding driftwood for the fires. We children took a sled and set out along the shore of the Beaufort Sea,

picking up bits and pieces. Sometimes we found
a piece of wood about three feet long, and carried
it home with pride. We also collected dwarf
willow branches. Wood was only used to start
the fire in the morning. Once we had it going
we heaped on seal oil, mixed with ashes. This
mixture threw out quite a lot of heat, but it had
a nasty odour until we got used to it. Sometimes
on their way home from the trap-lines, the men
brought coal that they had picked up. This was
not in solid lumps; it was chips and dust and
we had to use a lot of it to keep the house warm.
Still it was a change from going out to gather
driftwood.

During this time the men would be away on
their trap-lines for two to three weeks at a time.
They came home only to replenish their grub-
boxes and dump their furs. It was a busy time
for them. The fox furs were at their prime during
the winter months and the traps had to be visited
often. My family needed many furs to pay off
the debts they had taken on to make this trip
to Banks Island. There had to be money as well
to carry the family through the coming year.

While the men were away, the women skinned,
stretched and dried the pelts.

When my dad came home from his trips our

tent became a warm and happy place once more. It was too quiet while he was away, but when he returned it rang with laughter. He teased us all and played silly games with us. He told us stories too, and I would miss these while he was out on his trap-line. Every night when he was home, I would beg him to tell us a story at bed-time. There was one that he told that still stays clear in my mind. He said it was a true story.

"Long ago, when I was a younger man living at Cambridge Bay, I was out on my trap-line alone. One night after I made a snow-house, I happened to notice a white owl sitting on the coal-oil can. I thought that the heat inside, after a day of travelling in the cold, was giving me hallucinations. I closed my eyes and opened them again to see if the owl had disappeared. No, he was still there. I felt just a bit frightened. He blinked his eyes at me, unfolded his wings and flew through the walls of the snow-house. When I came back to the village a shaman named Akiko-miak told me exactly how many foxes I had brought back from the trip. I told him he was right, and asked him how he knew. He said, 'Remember the white owl that you thought you did not see in your igloo? That was me. I was watching you'."

After my father finished the story I asked "But Dad, how can a human turn into an owl?" He replied that there are many supernatural things that have no answer and it was best not to question them when they happened.

At Easter time my dad and my step-mother decided to go to Holman Island for staples. My brother and I would stay home with our grandparents and their family of four. While they were gone we carried on with our chores. We collected driftwood, and since the days were getting warmer, we ranged far afield in our search. The boys took a gun to shoot ptarmigan and for protection against polar bears, if we should meet one. When we finished our different chores, we played outside, sliding down from the top of the roof on the bank of snow that the winter winds had packed into a natural hill. Sometimes we dug a tunnel and made a room to play in under the slope. When we played outside on Banks Island we were constantly on the look-out for bears, and one day a bear did come. The dogs suddenly started to bark in a tone that was different to the sound they made at feeding time. My grandfather said "Nanook" and picked up his gun and went outside. Sure enough there was a bear heading towards the tents. Grandfather fired two shots

The men ice the runners of the sleds before they return to their trap-lines.

W. Gibson

and the bear fell. While he and the boys were skinning the bear we noticed that he had been hungry for a long time. There was no fat on him, and very little meat on his bones.

By this time we were down to our last can of bully beef and our last cup of rice, which we made into gruel for supper. We knew that we would not starve but a diet of ptarmigan could be monotonous. A few days later my grandfather shouted from the roof-top that a dog-team was coming. It was my dad and mother at last. We helped them unhitch and tie up the dogs. Then, with some exaggeration, we told our parents that we had nearly starved to death while we waited for them to bring in all the flour, tea, sugar and other things we were unloading from the sled. During supper they told of their trip to Holman Island. The best news was that the price of fox pelts had gone up.

Then the cleaning of the pelts began. We took the furs outside and rubbed cornmeal into them to rid them of yellowness; then we hung them on the clothes line to bleach in the sun. Soon the snow on the land melted. We put our boat back in the water, loaded it up, and weaving our way among the ice floes, we moved from our winter camp to a beautiful little inlet. We set the tents up on the gravel shore, with gentle rolling hills as a background.

Here we waited for the polar ice to leave the sea before we set out for Aklavik. The days were warm and we made the most of them by cooking and eating our meals outside. The sky was filled with ducks and geese coming back to nest. Once more we were living well off the land. Now instead of searching for driftwood we searched for duck eggs. We took only one or two from each nest for our food. Another spring meal that we had was a soup made from caribou leg-bones. We had eaten the marrow during the winter and had saved the bones until spring. We pounded them with rocks to break them up and boiled them in a big pot to get every last bit of goodness from them. After the broth cooled we had an inch or two of fat on top to eat with our sour dough bread. The caribou hooves were also made into a tasty soup. We skinned and boiled them until they were falling apart. Then we took them off the stove to cool, removed the toe-nails, added onions, rice and dehydrated vegetables and simmered the broth again. This may sound offensive because of the toe-nails, but it tasted good.

The spring sun shining on the waters of the bay and reflecting on the floating cakes of ice made a beautiful sight. The birds — eider ducks, old squaw ducks and loons — were all around us as we played outside on the tundra. Our noise did not seem to bother them. Out in the water the seals bobbed in and out among the floes. We kept the gramophone outside and when we saw a seal close we cranked up the gramophone and played a western song for it. The seal would be so curious it would come right in and stare at us with its big brown eyes.

The only thing that marred my happiness that spring was a chest cold that I could not seem to shake. My coughing started to bother grandma and she dosed me with her famous chewing-tobacco-juice remedy. It was bad enough to chew the plug of tobacco, but the thought of swallowing the juice made me break out in a sweat. I gagged a few times but I finally managed to get it down. Then it hit my system. The earth spun around so fast that I staggered and had to lie down until the spinning stopped. I decided that I would far rather have the cough than that kind of treatment every day.

On July 15 we loaded everything we owned and headed out for Aklavik. The landscape was magnificent. As we passed Nelson Head I saw a purple and blue cliff plunging down into the sea. I realized how much I had missed when we made the trip to Banks Island in the autumn. I made up my mind to stay on deck for the trip back.

One day we stopped for a few hours at the Smoky Mountains, named for the continual smoke that rose from the hills. The men dropped anchor and paddled to shore in canoes to climb the hills. While they were gone grandmother told us the legend of the *Innuakkotliguroaks* (little people). They were only twelve inches tall, she said, and they lived deep in the mountains. The smoke that we saw came from their cooking pots. Regardless of their size, they were able to capture caribou, rabbits or any game that they wished by making snares to trap them by the legs. When an animal was caught in a snare, they shot it with their small bows and arrows. As if to prove her story, the men brought back rocks shaped like little pots, bowls and plates. Grandmother said that this was the pottery they had made.

As we travelled on we came to Baillie Island. "This was your birthplace," my father told me. We went ashore and set out to explore the few remaining houses. He told us that when I was born, the place was a thriving community with many more buildings than we now saw. When we came close to them, we saw that the buildings were all at crazy angles from the ice shoving them to and fro each year.

About a mile away from the sandspit on a bank lived my father's adopted parents — Violet and Edward Kikoak, and their children Billy, Molly, Edward Jr., and Douglas. While we were exploring they came down to invite us up to the house for supper. Shortly after we had eaten, we said our goodbyes and headed on to Tuktoyaktuk and Aklavik.

When my father took the furs into The Bay store they sold at a good price. There was enough money to pay off last year's debts and to outfit my family for another year on Banks Island.

CHAPTER FOURTEEN

The last Years at School

MAINLY because I had been so sick during our stay at Banks Island last year I would not be making the return trip. Instead my father found a family at Aklavik who would board me for a year. Feeling unwanted and sad, I started to gather my things together. I asked my father who these people were that I would be staying with. He replied that they were a couple named Mr. and Mrs. Robinson. They had been married last year and now they had a small son, Robin. "Mr. Robinson works for the Department of Transport wireless station in Aklavik," Dad was saying as we came to the door and knocked on it. I felt uneasy, waiting for the knock to be answered. Then the door opened and there stood Miss Neville, my boarding-school supervisor, with a baby in her arms. She seemed pleased to see me and asked me to come right in. I felt a little better. At least she was not a stranger,

The Aklavik store and Dr. Livingstone's house, right.   H B C

I thought to myself. I said goodbye to my father at the door and followed her inside.

About the 21st of August, after I had been at Robinsons for a week, my father came to bid me a last farewell before he sailed. He took me out to supper and to a show at Peffer's Hotel and told me that he had arranged credit for me at The Bay store for the coming year. He assured me that the year would pass quickly, and that if all went well, he would see me next summer. He gave me a hug and a kiss and left me at the door. That was the last I saw of him for two years.

I settled down in my new home to help with the housework in the mornings and look after the baby in the afternoons. Our next door neighbours were Dr. and Mrs. L. D. Livingstone. He was the only doctor in Aklavik but the most surprising thing that he did was keep cows and chickens in a barn a mile beyond the Roman Catholic Mission. Donald, an Eskimo boy from my school, was the cowherd. Every morning he brought the five cows down from the barn and herded them through the settlement to find pasture. Sometimes a dog yelped at their heels and set off a stampede. People scattered in every direction to get out of the way of the run-away cows. Whenever I had Robin out for a walk and I saw Donald herding the cows to pasture, I gave them a wide berth. I found out how fast the cows could cover the ground during the first week of my stay with the Robinsons. I was taking the baby for his afternoon outing when I saw them galloping up behind us, covering the ground in a panic to get away from a barking dog. I also covered the ground fast that day. Poor Robin cried in indignation at being jostled around in his stroller during our mad rush for the yard and safety. I had seen cows in pictures, chewing on a clump of grass in a nice peaceful field. I had

always thought of them as beautiful, quiet creatures. It was much different being chased by them
in real life.

Each morning Mrs. Livingstone, a plump and
motherly sort of person, called "yahoo" to signal
that she had our fresh milk and eggs for breakfast.
When she passed them over the fence to me she
always took time to ask how I was and if I were
liking the milk any better. She knew that I was
having a hard time drinking it. I had had powdered and canned milk all my life and I found
that the taste of fresh milk was too much like
the smell of grass. Not wanting to hurt her feel-

'Buttercup,' Dr. Livingstone's Jersey heifer at Aklavik. The 'Distributor'
is in the background.

HBC

ings, I always answered "Yes" but I knew it would never be one of my favourite beverages.

When school started in September I went to afternoon classes only. My girl friends asked how it felt to be a "day schooler".

"Oh, it's not too bad, especially without you noisy girls around."

"I'll bet you wish you were back," they answered.

Still thinking of Mrs. Robinson in terms of being Miss Neville, I said "I don't mind living with Miss Neville. It's almost like living in school except that it's quiet at night and I miss all those scary stories we used to tell after lights out."

It really was not bad, living with the Robinsons, but I did get lonesome for my family and for the companionship of other children.

The winter months passed in the routine of looking after Robin in the mornings and going to school in the afternoons. In April the Robinsons were transferred and I was back in boarding school for the rest of the term. I knew the holidays were not too far away and that I would soon be seeing my parents, so I did not mind too much.

But when the time came for a summer vacation, my family did not come for me. I spent the holidays with my grandfather Okalisok and grandma Kakotok. They were at whaling camp and even though I had a good time while I was with them, I kept thinking of my father. They told me it would be another year before I would see him, and I felt miserable and discouraged. As far as I could see there was no hope of ever finishing school for good. I saw myself growing old in the years to come, still living out my life in the school dormitory. I went back with a heavy heart that year. In spite of my gloomy thoughts it was to be my last year in boarding school.

Summer came and went and I spent my fourteenth birthday in school. I'd spent half of my life there — seven years out of fourteen. Steeling myself for still another winter, I tried not to feel too unloved and unwanted by my father. I forgave him in my mind for the unforeseen problems that kept him away. Then one of the girls, coming in from the coast handed me a letter. It was from my father.

He began by calling me "Mom" for I was named for his mother and her spirit lived in me. Then he told me the good news. He was coming in to Aklavik to take me home in the early part of November. I was needed to take care of my younger sisters and to help with the household

Alice's father with his second wife. Unalena, and their family of four children.　　　　　　　　　　　　Collection: Alice French

chores. He said that we would be spending the winter in Napoyak.

I was going home for good. One part of my mind kept saying and believing this, but another part shrieked a warning that November was still a long way away. What if he did not come? By the time he finally arrived, I was a nervous wreck.

It was sad to say goodbye to my friends but at the same time I felt a great sense of relief, like a prisoner whose sentence was finally over. When the door closed behind me and my father I felt like a bird flying home to the vast open tundra.

INDEX

109

110